The Power Card Strategy 2.0

The Power Card Strategy 2.0

Using Special Interests to Motivate Children and Youth With Autism Spectrum Disorder

Elisa Gagnon, M.S., and Brenda Smith Myles, Ph.D.

11209 Strang Line Rd.
Lenexa, Kansas 66215
www.aapcpublishing.net

PUBLISHING

11209 Strang Line Rd.
Lenexa, Kansas 66215
www.aapcpublishing.net

Publisher's Cataloging-in-Publication

Names:	Gagnon, Elisa, author.	Myles, Brenda Smith, author.
Title:	The power card strategy 2.0 : using special interests to motivate children and youth with autism spectrum disorder / Elisa Gagnon, and Brenda Smith Myles.
Description:	[Second edition].	Lenexa, Kansas : AAPC Publishing, [2016]	Revised edition of: Power cards: using special interests to motivate children and youth with Asperger Syndrome and autism / Elisa Gagnon (Shawnee Mission, Kan. : Autism Asperger Pub., 2001).	Includes bibliographical references.
Identifiers:	ISBN: 978-1-942197-26-3	LCCN: 2016944672
Subjects:	LCSH: Autism spectrum disorders in children--Patients--Treatment.	Autistic children--Treatment.	Autistic children--Education--Social aspects--Study and teaching.	Social skills in children--Study and teaching.	Social interaction in children--Study and teaching.	Motivation in education.	Teachers of children with disabilities--Handbooks, manuals, etc.
Classification:	LCC: LC4717.5 .G34 2016	DDC: 618.92/85882--dc23

All art and photos ©BigStockPhotos

This book is designed in Cambria and Calibri.

Printed in the United States of America.

• • •
Table of Contents

• • •

Introduction to
the Second Edition

I am honored to be a part of the second edition of the Power Card book. Many researchers, parents, and autistics themselves have long understood the role of special interests in teaching and motivating individuals with autism spectrum disorder (ASD), yet these intense areas of knowledge have not been widely integrated into the learning activities of children on the spectrum. It was Elisa Gagnon's insightful and innovative Power Card Strategy that helped move the use of special interests forward – a gentle nudge as it were – promoting classroom-based research on the deep areas of knowledge and learners on the spectrum.

More recently, neurological research has supported the use of special interests. For example, Dichter, Felder, Green, Rittenberg, Sasson and Bodfish (2012) found that brain-based responses to monetary rewards was diminished for learners on the spectrum, whereas brain responses to special interests were intact. Similarly, analyzing children's brains, Cascio and colleagues (2014) discovered that children with ASD had an intact and *enhanced* brain-based response to special interests. Thus, there is significant evidence to suggest that special interests support the learning of individuals with ASD.

Elisa and I are hopeful that the second edition of this book will further inspire professionals and parents to incorporate special interests into the lives of learners on the spectrum.

– Brenda Smith Myles

Introduction to the First Edition

After many years of working with children and youth with autism spectrum disorder (ASD), it has become clear to me that these students need special supports to meet the challenges at home, at school, and in the community. As a teacher I have tried many things, among them visual supports (cf. Knight, Sartini, & Spriggs, 2015); social narratives (cf. Wright et al., 2016); structured teaching (cf. Mesibov & Shea, 2010); applied behavior analysis techniques (cf. Virués-Ortega, 2010); a variety of antecedent-based interventions (cf. Watkins, Kuhn, Ledbetter-Cho, Gevarter, & O'Reilly, 2015); self-management strategies (cf. Hampshire, Butera, & Bellini, 2016); social skills programs (cf. Kasari et al., 2016); sensory strategies (cf. Case-Smith, Weaver, & Fristad, 2014); and peer-implemented interventions (cf. Barber, Saffo, Gilpin, Craft, & Goldstein, 2016). Although these techniques, either alone or in combination, were successful with many of my students, I still felt that something was missing. I wasn't tapping into the strengths and interests of the children to help them learn and be motivated by learning. Thus, I began using a technique that does just that.

A strategy I called "Claudia's Cards" came out of a sense of desperation when Claudia refused to stay on task; in fact, she refused to do anything except sing the theme song from *Sesame Street* and talk about Big Bird. I gained her attention by reading a story I created myself entitled "Big Bird Learns to Stay on Task." After I had Claudia's attention, I provided her with a small card with a picture of Big Bird and simple instructions for staying on task. I soon realized that Claudia would do things for Big Bird that she would never consider doing for me. I began using "Claudia's Cards" successfully with other children.

As I used this technique with students and saw the positive results, I thought that other teachers and parents might also find success with "Claudia's Cards." However, I felt that the technique needed an "official" name that would better describe what it was. After much deliberation, I decided that what I was doing was best described by the term "Power Card Strategy." Briefly, the Power Card Strategy is a visual aid developed by educators and parents to assist students with ASD in making sense of social situations, routines, the meaning of language, and the hidden curriculum that surrounds us wherever we go. What sets the Power Card Strategy apart is that it makes use of children's special interests – one of the unique characteristics of children with ASD – to help them make sense of situations they encounter on a daily basis.

In short, a brief scenario was used to explain how the hero or special interest has encountered and solved a problem the student herself is facing. Then a card (typically the size of a trading card or business card) is created that summarizes the strategy and contains a picture of the special interest/hero. The child carries this card with her as a reminder when similar situations come up.

• • •
How to Use This Book

This book starts out with a discussion of the role of special interests in the lives of those on the spectrum, the foundation of the Power Card strategy, along with a discussion of the growing research supporting this powerful strategy. The strategy and its uses are described in Chapter 2 with step-by-step directions for creating Power Cards, again with an emphasis on the underlying research. Chapter 3 presents novel ways to integrate special interests into home and school settings to support regulation, communication, and other daily skills. Chapter 4 provides samples of how the Power Card strategy has been used to increase academic performance. Throughout, application of the Power Card strategies is illustrated in both general and special education settings, with students of varying ages and skill levels.

The Power Card strategy is NOT appropriate for every child with ASD. For example, it may not be appropriate for a child severely impacted with autism, nor may it be appropriate for a child with extremely low motivation. The appropriateness of using the Power Card strategy, like all teaching techniques, must be evaluated for each individual child.

I hope you meet with the same success that we have enjoyed using the Power Card strategy.

– Elisa Gagnon

Please note the citations in the original introduction have been updated to further validate the strategy and demonstrate the ongoing interest in this important topic.

• • •
CHAPTER 1

Special Interests and Autism Spectrum Disorder

Individuals with autism spectrum disorder (ASD) have limitless potential, and tapping into and realizing that potential is largely dependent on those who support them. That is, we know that individuals with ASD can learn and exhibit skills that we originally thought improbable or impossible – *when they are taught to do so.*

To meet the instructional needs of students on the spectrum, researchers have identified effective teaching practices – the *how* to teach (Centers for Medicare & Medicaid Services [CMS], 2010; National Autism Center [NAC] (2015); National Professional Development Center on ASD [NPDC], n.d.). Unfortunately, to date, less emphasis has been placed on *making instruction meaningful* despite empirical evidence that provides significant direction in this regard. Namely, researchers have repeatedly found that incorporating special interests into instruction can positively impact learners on the spectrum.

This information is not new. Indeed, one of the first observations about individuals with ASD focused on their intense areas of interest. For example, Hans Asperger (1944/1991), observing his patients, recognized the power of special interests, stating that they enable "them to achieve quite extraordinary levels of performance in a certain area" (p. 45).

· · ·

Definition of Special Interests

Special interests are intense, sometimes all-consuming, hobbies or areas of expertise. Often referred to as circumscribed or restricted interests, they can include common topics, such as video games or movies, or unique subjects, given the individual's age and the context, such as solar energy or pythons (Cascio et al., 2014; Mercier, Mottron, & Belleville, 2000; Turner-Brown, Lam, Holtzclaw, Dichter, & Bodfish, 2011).

Boyd, Conroy, Mancil, Nakao, and Alter (2007) identified four defining characteristics of special interests:

- Accumulation of large amount of information
- Difficulty redirecting the individual from physically interacting with or conversing about the interest
- Lengthy duration of fascination with the interest
- Intensity of engagement with the interest

Special interests often do not lessen with age (Fecteau et al., 2003). In fact, the number of a child's interests may increase as he or she approaches adulthood (Bashe & Kirby, 2010).

Special interests have been further described as primary and secondary.

A **primary special interest** is one where the student demonstrates an all-encompassing level of interest in a particular topic to such an extent that a discussion of this topic can escalate to almost meltdown behavior, where the student cannot control his discussion of the topic and behavior. Rapid speech, increased volume, a high-pitched voice, pacing, and hand wringing often occur with primary obsessions.

Primary special interests typically do not lend themselves to rational discussions and explorations. Indeed, students who have this type of obsession seem to discuss the topic in an almost circular fashion. However, over time primary interests can transform in secondary special interests (Myles & Simpson, 2003).

A secondary interest is a marked interest about which the student remains lucid, focused, and ready to learn about the particular topic. Students actively seek new information about the topic but can be redirected.

Secondary interests are often used by teachers and families to motivate students to complete academic and social tasks. In some cases, secondary obsessions develop into career interests (Myles & Simpson, 2003).

The focus of this book is on secondary special interests.

Marco has an intense interest in silent movies. When he watches silent movies or talks about the filming of these movies, he becomes animated and almost frantic, talking rapidly about this interest. Further, it is extremely difficult to redirect him from this topic, and attempts to do so often result in meltdowns. Marco is also very interested in super heroes, talking about them frequently. However, as opposed to silent movies, he can easily be encouraged to change that topic of conversation.

For Marco, silent movies are a primary special interest that should not be integrated into his school assignments. His secondary intense interest in super heroes, however, lends itself well to be used at home and school.

• • •

Prevalence of Special Interests

Between 75% (Klin, Danovitch, Merz, & Volkmar, 2007) and 90% (Bashe & Kirby, 2010) of individuals on the spectrum develop deep and intense interests compared to 30% of their neurotypical peers. These special interests may occur as early as 1 to 2 years of age and last throughout the lifespan (DeLoache, Simcock, & Macari, 2007; Jordan & Caldwell-Harris, 2012), often increasing in adulthood (Boyd et al., 2007). Adults with ASD report that they spend an average of 26 hours per week on their special interest and have a high level of proficiency in that area (Kirchner & Dziobek, 2014).

• • •

Areas of Special interests

Areas of special interest vary across individuals with ASD, but the most frequent areas of focus include (a) transportation, (b) machines and technology, (c) dinosaurs, (d) history and culture, (e) video games, (f) sports, (g) people, (h) science, (i) sports and games, (j) animals, (k) art, and (l) motion pictures. The special interests of boys on the spectrum are often different from those of their neurotypical peers. However, the interests of girls tend to mirror those of their same-age, same-gender peers with an emphasis on (a) animals, (b) books, (c) art, (d) dress-up, (e) nature, (f) music, and (g) movies (DeLoache et al., 2007; Jordan & Caldwell-Harris, 2012; Winter-Messiers, 2007).

Despite the frequency of the above areas of interest, many children and adolescents on the spectrum have interests that are not based on these categories but are distinctly unique – often referred to as idiosyncratic. Examples include medieval dress, constructing imaginative objects, brooms, and bodily injuries (DeLoache et al., 2007).

• • •

The Power of Special Interests: Learning

The power of special interests, referred to as Restricted Patterns of Behavior and Interests under the classification of autism spectrum disorder in the *Diagnostic and Statistical Manual of Mental Disorders* (American Psychiatric Associations [APA], 2013), in the lives of those on the spectrum should not be underestimated. As shown in Table 1, deep and intense interests have been found to have a positive outcome.

Table 1

Positive Outcomes for Individuals With ASD When Special Interests Are Incorporated Into Learning and Behavior Activities

Outcome Area	Selected Citations
Social interaction	Boyd et al. (2007); Dunst, Trivette, & Masiello (2011); Jung & Sainato (2015); Koegel, Kim, Koegel, & Schwartzman (2013)
Joint attention	Kryzak, Bauer, Jones, & Sturmey (2013); Vismara & Lyons (2007); White et al. (2011)
Pretend play	Kryzak et al. (2013); Porter (2012)
Self-confidence	Winter-Messiers (2007)
Language development	Vismara & Lyons (2007)
Communication	Davis, Boon, Cihak, & Fore (2010); Spencer, Simpson, Day, & Buster (2008)
Sportsmanship	Keeling, Myles, Gagnon, & Simpson (2003)
Decreased anxiety	Wood et al. (2009)
Decreased behavior problems	Lanou, Hough, & Powell (2012)
Visual exploration	Sasson, Elison, Turner-Brown, Dichter, & Bodfish (2011)
Perspective taking	Lanou et al. (2012)
Motivation	Gunn & Delafield (2015)
Direction following	Campbell & Tincani (2011)
Conversation	Davis et al. (2010)
Task engagement	El Zein, Solis, Lang, & Kim (2014)
Academic performance	Mancil & Pearl (2008); Jung & Sainato (2015)
Reading comprehension	El Zein et al. (2014)
Productivity	Koegel, Singh, & Koegel (2010)
Correct responses	Vismara & Lyons (2007)

Note. The above citations are marked with an asterisk in the References.

• • •

The Power of Special Interests:
Its Importance to Individuals With ASD

Winter-Messiers and colleagues (2007) interviewed 23 children, adolescents, and young adults on the spectrum about the role their special interests played in their lives. Overall, respondents reported that the world made more sense and they felt a greater sense of confidence and positivity when engaged with their areas of special interest.

Figure 1 highlights the positive aspects of special interests for those who participated in the study.

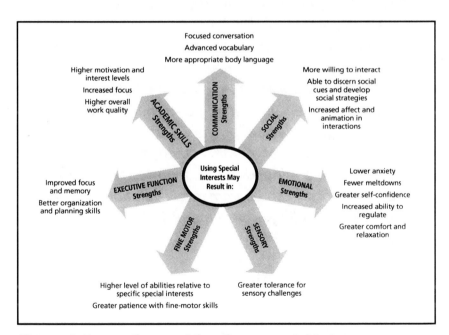

Figure 1. **Strengths resulting from special interests.**

Adapted from Winter-Messiers, M. A., Herr, C. M., Wood, C. E., Brooks, A. P., Gates, A.M.A., Houston, T. L., & Tingstad, K. I. (2007). How far can Brian ride the Daylight 4449 Express: A strength-based model of Asperger syndrome based on special interest areas. *Focus on Autism and Other Developmental Disabilities, 22*(2), 67-79.

• • •

Summary

Clearly, special interests are important to and positively impact children, adolescents, and adults on the spectrum. As such, they should be incorporated into their day whenever possible – in particular, into assignments and reinforcement systems.

The next chapter introduces the Power Card strategy, a meaningful way to teach and support the use of social/communication, academic, and self-regulation skills.

> *Able autistic individuals can rise to eminent positions and perform with such outstanding success that one may even conclude that only such people are capable of certain achievements. It is as if they had compensatory abilities to counterbalance their deficiencies. Their unswerving determination and penetrating intellectual powers, part of their spontaneous and original mental activity, their narrowness and single-mindedness, as manifested in their special interests, can be immensely valuable and can lead to outstanding achievements in their chosen areas.* (Asperger, 1944/1991, p. 88)

CHAPTER 2

Developing and Using the Power Card Strategy

B ased on the 27 focused interventions identified through scientific research to be effective when implemented correctly with students with ASD (CMS, 2010; NAC, 2015; NPDC, n.d.), the Power Card strategy is an evidence-based practice under the categories of antecedent-based interventions and visual supports (CMS, NAC, NPDC). This unique type of visual aid incorporates the child's special interest in teaching appropriate social interactions, including routines, behavior expectations, the meaning of language, and the hidden curriculum (cf. Myles, Endow, & Mayfield, 2013; Myles, Trautman, & Schelvan, 2013; Myles & Kolar, 2013).

• • •

Research on the Power Card Strategy

To date, six studies have been conducted on the effectiveness of the Power Card strategy. As a result of using this strategy, children and adolescents on the spectrum between the ages of 5 and 17 years of age experienced the following significant gains: (a) reduced screaming and whining while playing games (Keeling et al., 2003); (b) increased time engaged with peers (Spencer et al., 2008);

(c) increased conversational skills (Davis, Boon, Cihak, & Fore, 2010); (d) increased direction following (Campbell & Tincani, 2011); (e) decreased time needed to transition between activities (Angell, Nicholson, Watts, & Blum, 2011); and (f) increased turn-taking (Daubert, Hornstein, & Tincani, 2015).

• • •

Power Card Overview

Briefly, the Power Card strategy consists of presenting – on a single sheet or in booklet form – a short scenario, written in the first person, that describes how the child's hero solves a problem, along with a small card, the Power Card, that recaps how the learner can use the same strategy to solve a similar problem herself.

The hero or special interest serves several purposes.

- The underlying purpose is to serve as a motivator. Students with ASD most often "tune in" when their special interest is mentioned.

- Using the special interest is nonthreatening. Students on the spectrum often find it easier to buy into this sort of scenario than follow a top-down command of "Here's what you have to do."

- The Power Card strategy capitalizes on the "relationship" between the child and the hero or role model. Since the child wants to be like his hero, he is more likely to do what the hero suggests.

• • •

Power Card Example

Gary, a 9-year-old on the spectrum, was very enthusiastic about answering every question the teacher asked whether or not it was directed at him. He often blurted a response or interrupted other students who were trying to respond to the teacher.

Gary's special interest was Angry Birds. Using the basic principles behind the Power Card strategy, the following scenario was developed based on Gary's special interest and the target behavior (difficulty waiting his turn).

The Angry Birds Learn to Wait Their Turn

Before they are able to join the Angry Birds, the birds had to go to school and learn how to be part of the team. The red bird had a particularly hard time learning to wait his turn. He wanted to answer all of the questions. When the teacher asked the group a question, he sometimes shouted out the answer without raising his hand. The blue bird, the white bird, and the black bird often became upset that the red bird was not following the classroom rule about waiting his turn.

The Angry Birds' teacher taught the red bird these four steps:
1. *Listen to the question.*
2. *Think to yourself, "Do I have an answer?"*
3. *If you have an answer, raise your hand. Don't speak unless the teacher calls your name.*
4. *If the teacher calls on you, answer the question.*

Just like the red bird, you can be part of the Angry Bird team. Being a part of the team will make all of the Angry Birds happy. They will be happy that you are on their team!

In the first paragraph of the scenario, Gary learns that in order for his heroes to be part of the team, they had to learn how to answer questions. The second paragraph encourages Gary to try to answer questions using the Angry Bird's four steps. Gary was encouraged to practice the replacement behavior several times and was verbally praised for "answering questions just like the Angry Birds Team."

After Gary was introduced to the scenario, he was given the Power Card. About the size of a business card, the Power Card consists of a picture related to the Angry Birds and the steps that Gary needs to remember when answering questions.

The Angry Birds follow these four steps to answer questions

1. **Listen to the question.**
2. **Think to yourself, "Do I have an answer?"**
3. **If you have an answer, raise your hand. Don't speak unless the teacher calls your name.**
4. **If the teacher calls on you, answer the question.**

• • •

Components of the Power Card Strategy

To be effective, the Power Card Strategy must include the two main elements just illustrated in Gary's case.

1. **A *brief scenario* using the student's hero or special interest and the behavior or situation that is difficult for him.** In the first paragraph, the hero or role model attempts a solution to the problem and experiences success. The second paragraph encourages the student to try out the new behavior, which is broken down into three to five manageable steps.

   The scenario is written at the student's comprehension level. For example, a scenario for a high school student with ASD might be written on a single page in paragraph form. For an elementary student, it might be written in a large font over several pages with pictures of the special interest throughout. Relevant pictures or graphics include magazine pictures, computer-generated photographs downloaded from the Internet, teacher drawings, student drawings, or icons.

2. **The *Power Card,* which is the size of a trading card, bookmark, or business card.** The card contains a small picture of the special interest and the solutions to the problem behavior or situation broken down into three to five steps. The Power Card is provided to aid in generalization. It can be carried in a purse, wallet, or pocket; be velcroed® inside a book, notebook, or locker;

placed on the corner of a student's desk; or presented on a smartphone or tablet, such as an iPad.

• • •

Where and When to Use the Power Card Strategy

The Power Card strategy is appropriate for behaviors or situations in which the learner on the spectrum:

- Lacks understanding of what to do, such as hidden curriculum items, routines, or language use that the student has not been taught.
- Does not understand that he has choices.
- Has difficulty understanding that there is a cause-and-effect relationship between a specific behavior and its consequence.
- Has difficulty remembering what to do without a prompt.
- Does not understand the perspective of others.
- Knows what to do when calm but cannot follow a given routine under stress.
- Needs a visual reminder to recall the behavioral expectation for a situation.
- Has difficulty generalizing.
- Is difficult to motivate and may be motivated only by the special interest.
- Has difficulty accepting directions from an adult.

The Power Card strategy is usually NOT appropriate when the learner with ASD:

- Has sensory needs such as difficulty tolerating certain noises, smells, or tastes. Although the strategy can help somebody realize that they may be experiencing a need for sensory input, it will not by itself satisfy that need. However, it may bring about a slight delay by reminding the learner what she needs to do to get her needs met.

- Is extremely challenged cognitively and appears not to understand spoken language at the sentence or paragraph level. To use the Power Card strategy, the child, adolescent, or adult does not have to be a reader if pictures or graphics are used to explain the problem situation or behavior and a supportive adult serves as the reader.

- Engages in the problem behavior only once. It is difficult to determine a cause or motivation for a behavior unless it occurs somewhat frequently.

- Does not share a positive relationship with the adult who is implementing the strategy. Remember, the Power Card strategy is not a punishment. It should not be perceived as negative in any way. It is fulfilling a need for the individual while capitalizing on his special interest.

- Is in crisis. When the child is experiencing a meltdown (Myles & Aspy, 2016), this technique will not work. Since the person on the spectrum is not functioning at her optimal level, she cannot make rational decisions. Worse yet, using the Power Card strategy during a meltdown will make this technique less effective at times when it is otherwise appropriate.

- Does not have a well-developed area of interest. In order to buy into the strategy, the student must want to follow the hero's/role model's directions.

• • •

The Steps in Using the Power Card Strategy

For any strategy to be effective, it is important to consider the individual needs of the student and create a plan accordingly. Sometimes a teacher or parent will say, "I tried that and it didn't work," when in reality they had invested very little time in developing and carrying out the plan.

The following steps are suggested to ensure optimal success.

1. **Identify the problem behavior or situation.** Select the behavior or situation and state it clearly. It is important to address only one behavior at a time.

2. **Identify the special interest.** In many cases, an area of interest is already obvious. If not, consider using a reinforcement survey or talk with the child or youth to determine an area of interest.

3. **Conduct a functional assessment.** The purpose of a functional assessment is to determine the reason or trigger for a particular problem behavior. Researchers and practitioners have developed a list of possible behavior functions or triggers, which include (a) escape/avoidance; (b) attention from peers or adults; (c) expression of anger or stress; (d) emotional state such as depression, frustration, and confusion; (e) power or control; (f) intimidation; (g) sensory stimulation; (h)

fear or relief of fear; (i) request to obtain something such as food, activity, object, comfort, routine, social interaction; or (j) expression of internal stimulation (i.e., sinus pain, skin irritation, hunger).

Other triggers commonly found among children and youth with ASD include (a) obsessional thoughts, (b) fear of failure, (c) fear related to self-esteem, and (d) lack of understanding behavioral expectations, routines, or commands (Matson & Nebel-Schwalm, 2007; Myles & Aspy, 2016; Reese, Richman, Belmont, & Morse, 2005).

School personnel may elect to use one of many commercially developed functional assessment instruments such as *FBA to Z: Functional Behavior and Intervention Plans for Individuals With ASD* (Aspy, Grossman, Myles, & Henry, 2016), which targets the underlying characteristics of ASD that are related to behavior challenges by going beyond a focus on the antecedent-behavior-consequence (ABC) patterns in a reductionistic manner; the *Motivation Assessment Scale* (Durand & Crimmins, 1992), which identifies the functions of challenging behavior as (a) sensory, (b) escape, (c) attention, or (d) tangible; or the *Student-Assisted Functional Assessment Interview* (Kern, Dunlap, Clarke, & Childs, 1994), which poses open- and closed-ended questions.

Many school districts develop their own instruments, which take into account their school environment and culture in addition to the special characteristics of children and youth with ASD.

4. **Determine whether the Power Card strategy is an appropriate intervention.** As mentioned earlier, there are many situations in which the Power Card strategy will work and many behavioral functions for which it is

effective. However, there are also many situations and functions for which it will not work. Therefore, determining whether the Power Card strategy is an appropriate intervention is an important step.

Sometimes, on the surface, the strategy may not appear to be the best intervention; however, a closer analysis will reveal that it would indeed help the student. For example, if a child loses control because of stress and anxiety, the strategy will not relieve that stress. However, it can help prompt the child to get to a safe place to de-stress or get sensory input, if that is what she needs. Similarly, if a student wants to escape/avoid the lunchroom, the Power Card strategy will probably not reduce that desire or need. However, it can provide him with an alternative and acceptable way to meet this need. In this case, the strategy could prompt the student to ask the lunch attendant for permission to take his lunch to the resource room to eat with a small group.

5. **Collect baseline data.** Collecting data over several days enables you to determine a pattern of behavior. Baseline data collection typically spans three to five days, but in some cases it might need to be longer to ensure that enough appropriate information has been gathered. No elaborate system is required. A behavior may be measured by simply placing tally marks on a sheet of paper each time the behavior occurs or by using a stopwatch to record the length of time a behavior occurs.

6. **Write the scenario and design the Power Card.** The scenario and the Power Card should be written in accordance with the student's comprehension skills, using vocabulary and print size individualized for each student. The scenario is written in the first person and

either in the present (to describe a situation as it occurs) or the future tense (to anticipate an upcoming event). The first paragraph of the scenario relates to the "hero" or special interest, followed by a section that provides a solution to the problem. This solution is then applied to the child or youth's particular situation.

7. **Introduce the scenario and Power Card.** Before writing the scenario and the Power Card, an adult who has a positive rapport with the learner discusses how the Power Card Strategy works in general and how it will work with the student.

   After the scenario and Power Card are written, the adult or student read it together. This initial read-through should be followed by a discussion. Further, the student who is able to read independently should be encouraged to read the scenario and Power Card to other significant adults or peers so that everybody has a similar perspective of the problem situation and appropriate behaviors.

8. **Collect intervention data to determine effectiveness.** Data should be collected throughout the intervention process using the same procedures as when gathering baseline data.

9. **Evaluate the intervention and make modifications, if needed.** If the data suggest that the desired changes have not occurred after implementing the intervention for two weeks, review the scenario and Power Card and the implementation procedures. If you decide to make alterations, it is recommended that only one variable is changed at a time. For example, start by changing the content of the scenario, rather than simultane-

ously changing the time when the scenario is read *and* the person who reads it. By changing only one factor at a time, you can determine the factor or factors that best facilitate learning.

10. **Empower the learner to determine how long to keep using the Power Card strategy.** Frequent verbal reinforcement will help the student understand that she has the skills necessary to maintain the appropriate behavior. When the child or youth internalizes the appropriate response, she is ready to perform the skill on a consistent basis.

11. **Based on learner input and performance, fade reading of the scenario while still keeping the Power Card.** Decisions on when to fade the scenario will vary based on individual needs. It is better to fade too late than too early. In fact, we recommend that the learner be given the control in determining when a given scenario is no longer needed.

12. **Based on learner input and performance, fade the use of the Power Card.** Again, individuals with ASD should be empowered to decide when and if to fade use of the Power Card. Too often we are tempted to pull back on the use of a strategy when we see the youth being successful. Remember, the learner is being successful because she has learned how to use the Power Card. Therefore, careful consideration must be given before removing it.

> *Some students want to retain the Power Card even though they refer to it infrequently. This should be allowed and even encouraged, if the student perceives it as providing support.*

• • •

Using the Power Card Strategy at Home and in the Community

Besides school, the Power Card strategy can be used at home and in the community, but chances are that all 12 steps just outlined are not necessary in those settings. Since parents are familiar with their child's special interest and needs, deciding how to use the strategy is easier.

Some questions to ask when selecting a behavior for change are:

1. Will the Power Card strategy make a significant difference in my child's and my family's life?

2. Will this make my child feel better about herself?

3. Will the strategy give my child independence?

4. Is it important to my child and my family that this behavior be addressed?

If parents answer "yes" to any of these questions, the behavior is probably one that should be addressed by this strategy or some other method.

While some parents may produce sophisticated computer-generated scenarios and Power Cards, we have found that the strategy is also effective when handwritten. Parents and their children can cut pictures from magazines, take photographs, download images from the Internet, or draw a special interest. The Power Card can be cut from construction paper or file folder material. One parent whose child's special interest was Batman photographed her son at Halloween in his Batman costume and used that picture on both the scenario and the Power Card.

Once you try the Power Card strategy, how do you know if it works? Maybe you will notice changes such as:

- Your child is having fewer meltdowns. Children often experience meltdowns because they do not know how to do something or how to get their needs met. The strategy may help the child understand or get something he needs.

- Your child has learned new and more positive behaviors.

- You as a parent feel less stressed.

- It feels easier for you and your child to be at home and to go out in the community together.

• • •

Summary

The Power Card strategy is a technique that may help children and youth with ASD function more appropriately and more comfortably at school, home, and in the community. By using a special interest, the child is motivated to use the strategy presented in the scenario and on the Power Card. Generalization is programmed through the Power Card to ensure that the identified behavior does not occur in just one environment.

This positive strategy is often entertaining for the child and is inexpensive and relatively simple to develop. The Power Card strategy can make a difference in the lives of many individuals with ASD and those who teach them and love them.

CHAPTER 3

Power Card Examples

This chapter contains scenarios and Power Card that have been used successfully with children and youth with ASD. Each example briefly describes a child or youth, his or her special interest, a target behavior, and the Power Card strategy used to meet the student's needs.

The Power Card samples include photos, line drawings, material downloaded from the Internet, etc. This is done to illustrate the range of materials that may be used so long as the special interest or other motivator is featured prominently. (Note: For copyright reasons, we are not able to use copyrighted or trade-marked materials, but this is an option for private use.) Samples are organized by the areas addressed in the Power Card scenarios and Power Cards as follows: (a) communication, (b) regulation, (c) school-based skills, and (d) home-based skills.

• • •

Communication

Mikashelle

Attending to adult directions has always been a challenge for Mikashelle. Her teachers and parents developed many interventions and supports to teach and reinforce this skill. Through a functional behavior assessment (FBA),

Mikashelle's team found that she has the skills to attend and listen but was either (a) not motivated to listen or (b) did not realize the importance. The Power Card strategy was implemented to address these issues. Mikashelle likes Hannah Montana on the Disney Channel.

Hannah Montana Pays Attention

Hannah Montana loves being in concert and also loves being on the set of her TV show. However, she still has to go to school. Sometimes it is hard for her to pay attention to her teachers when she is in class. As Miley Cyrus she is sometimes tempted to daydream about her other life as Hannah Montana. She has learned, however, that listening to her teachers and doing her school work is as important as singing, dancing, and acting. She has learned that she needs to pay attention in class and do her work so that she has time to do what she loves to do.

Just like Hannah Montana, it is important to pay attention in class. This would make Hannah Montana proud. Hannah would like all girls who love her to remember these three things:

1. *Listen to your teacher when she is talking. Be ready to answer any questions that she might ask.*

2. *Do your school assignments and stay on task until the assignment is complete.*

3. *Always ask for help when needed.*

Remember to pay attention in class and do your school work. You will have lots of time to watch and listen to Hannah Montana when you are finished.

1. **Listen to your teacher when she is talking. Be ready to answer any questions that she might ask.**
2. **Do your school assignments and stay on task until the assignment is complete.**
3. **Always ask for help when needed.**

Toby

Toby's use of profanity was impacting him negatively at home, school, and in the community. He was even given a written warning at his weekend job at the movie theater for using inappropriate language. To change his behavior, Toby's teacher decided to implement the Power Card strategy using one of his favorite Minion characters.

Carl the Minion Wants to Eliminate Profanity
with Kim Hanson

Carl is a yellow Minion with great potential to become a super leader in the Minion world, but he had a problem. Carl used profanity, also known as swearing or cursing, when he was at school and with his friends. The adults in his life, including his parents, his grandparents, and his teachers, did not like this behavior. They frequently asked him why he did this. Carl's response was "I don't know" or "To get attention from friends."

The adults were worried that if Carl did not stop cursing, he would never be able to reach his potential as a Minion leader. They were also afraid that he would turn purple. At first, Carl thought it might be fun to be a bad purple Minion even though he knew he would be letting down those who cared about him.

Sometimes when Carl cursed, his friends would laugh. This made Carl think that his friends thought he was funny. Sometimes his friends would tell adults that Carl was cursing, but he thought that this was not a big deal as long as he was getting attention. His friends were getting worried because they knew that Carl could be a great leader only if he stopped cursing. Minion leaders don't curse!

The parents of Carl's friends heard about Carl's use of curse words and decided that they didn't want Carl around their children. Carl's friends were not permitted to go to his birthday party or to sit with him at lunch anymore. Carl knew he had to act!

Carl first had to admit that the cursing had become a bad habit. He talked to his teacher about a plan to help him stop cursing. Here is the plan:

- Apologize to friends, teachers, and family for cursing in the past. Let them know that I will no longer use these words.

- Talk to my teacher and mom about words that are inappropriate and appropriate. Come up with a list of words to say instead.

- *If I feel like saying a curse word, I can say it in my head rather than saying it out loud. I don't have to say every word that comes into my head.*

When Carl quit using the curse words, his friends told their parents. Carl was once again included in activities and was on the right track to become a Minion leader!

- **Apologize to friends, teachers, and family for cursing in the past. Let them know that I will no longer use these words.**
- **Talk to my teacher and mom about words that are inappropriate and appropriate. Come up with a list of words to say instead.**
- **If I feel like saying a curse word, I can say it in my head rather than saying it out loud. I don't have to say every word that comes into my head.**

I will ask myself, "Is my behavior yellow or purple Minion behavior?"

Suzy

Suzy is a 12-year-old girl with ASD who frequently uses inappropriate and insulting language with her peers. She continually says exactly what is on her mind, with comments, such as "You have bad breath" or "Your hair looks terrible today." It is especially difficult for Suzy to be nice to people when she is tired or under stress. When her parents or teachers discuss this with her, she says that she is merely telling the truth or that she is tired and shouldn't have to be nice to people when she is tired. She cannot see the connection between her lack of friends and the way she speaks to others.

Suzy is a fan of Britney Spears and enjoys her music. Using the following scenario and Power Card decreased the occurrence of rude comments Suzy made to others.

Britney and Her Fans
by Cassie Jones

Britney Spears loves being a music star, but sometimes it is difficult for her to be nice to everyone. At the end of a long day in the recording studio or after a concert, she is often tired and it is difficult for her to be nice to her fans and friends. But Britney has learned that it is important to smile at people she meets and say nice things to everyone even when she is tired. She has learned that if she can't say something nice, it is better to just smile and say nothing at all. She stops and thinks about comments she makes before she says anything.

Just like Britney, it is important for young people to think before they talk. It makes Britney proud when preteens and teenagers remember to do the following:

1. *Think before you say anything. Say it in your head first before saying it out loud.*

2. *If you can't think of something nice to say, don't say anything.*

3. *You do not have to say every thought out loud that you think.*

1. **Think before you say anything. Say it in your head first before saying it out loud.**

2. **If you can't think of something nice to say, don't say anything.**

3. **You do not have to say every thought out loud that you think.**

Noki

Noki loved to hug people – whether she knew them or not. The following scenario and Power Card, using Noki's special interest, Justin Bieber, was implemented after a series of lessons about family and others, familiar and unfamiliar people, and greetings.

Justin Bieber's Rules for Hugging
by Julie Irvine

Justin Bieber loves being a star, but sometimes it is hard for him to be in the spotlight all of the time. In public, girls frequently try to hug him. Even though he doesn't want to hurt anyone's feelings, this makes him uncomfortable. He prefers when girls wave and say "hi."

Justin has very strict standards regarding hugging. He learned the rules for hugging when he was in middle school and would like all middle school students to apply these rules.

1. *Hugging is for families. It is not appropriate to hug teachers or students at school.*

2. *If you want to greet someone, it is better to say "hi" and smile.*

3. *It is not okay to hug anyone at school even on their birthday.*

Remember these three rules, and Justin will know that you are a true fan!

1. **Hugging is for families. It is not appropriate to hug teachers or students at school.**

2. **If you want to greet someone, it is better to say "hi" and smile.**

3. **It is not okay to hug anyone at school even on their birthday.**

Greg

Greg is an 11-year-old boy who is prompt-dependent throughout the school day, looking to his teacher or para-professionals to provide him with every instruction. Greg is interested in cartoon videos, and his parents report that his favorite video is *Charlotte's Web*. The following scenario and Power Card were developed to help Greg become more independent.

Wilbur Takes Charge
by Cindy Van Horn

Charlotte the spider loves her best friend, Wilbur the pig. Lately, Charlotte has been frustrated with Wilbur because he will not do anything unless she tells him what to do. Wilbur will not eat unless Charlotte tells him it is time to eat. Wilbur will not clean his pigpen unless Charlotte tells him to clean it. In fact, Wilbur won't even play with the other pigs unless Charlotte tells him it's time to play. Charlotte is tired! She knows Wilbur will be a happier pig if he asks for help instead of always having to be told what to do.

Just like Wilbur, it is important for all boys at school to be independent. It is important to do your work on your own without someone telling you what to do. If you don't know what to do, it is OK to ask for help. For example, boys can go through the lunch line by themselves without someone telling them every step they need to take. Of course, boys can always ask for help if they need it. Charlotte has decided she is going to wait for Wilbur to ask for help instead of always telling him what to do. She wants Wilbur to take charge!

Just remember Charlotte's three rules for taking charge:

1. *If you are not sure what to do, check your schedule.*

2. *Don't wait for someone to tell you what to do. Just do it!!*

3. *If you need help say, "I need help."*

Remember these three things and you can take charge just like Wilbur!

1. **If you are not sure what to do, check your schedule.**

2. **Don't wait for someone to tell you what to do. Just do it!!**

3. **If you need help say, "I need help."**

Minnie

Minnie is a 7-year-old girl, who spends much of the time in class laughing even when others do not understand why she is laughing. The high-pitched sound of her giggles is distracting and upsetting to some of her peers. Minnie does not read social cues, including the "teacher look," and responds to such looks by giggling even louder.

Minnie is very attached to her Minnie Mouse doll and insists on carrying it with her most of the time. She constantly points to the doll's pink shoes saying the words "pink shoes." This behavior occurs up to 100 times in a school day.

The classroom teacher wrote the following scenario and Power Card in conjunction with a behavior intervention plan in hopes of reducing Minnie's giggling at school. Since Minnie has not learned to read, her Power Card is two-sided with a picture of Minnie Mouse's pink shoes on one side and a quiet mouth icon on the reverse side.

Minnie Mouse and the Pink Shoes

Minnie Mouse loves to wear her pink shoes. She thinks her pink shoes are the most beautiful shoes in the world. Sometimes Mickey Mouse says to her, "Minnie, I just love your shoes." Just like Minnie Mouse, girls with quiet mouths at school can wear pink shoes. To get pink shoes, girls need to say, "I want pink shoes" to their teacher.

It is important to have a quiet mouth at school. It is okay to talk in a quiet voice, but giggling all the time is not okay.

Minnie Mouse wants all girls who love pink shoes to remember these three things:

1. *Say "I want pink shoes" to your teacher.*

2. *Have a quiet mouth (no giggling).*

3. *Look at your shoes or your Minnie Card to remember the rule.*

Remember to have a quiet mouth and you can have pink shoes just like Minnie!*

*This scenario was more effective in a booklet form with illustrations.

1. **Say "I want pink shoes" to your teacher.**
2. **Have a quiet mouth (no giggling).**
3. **Look at your shoes or your Minnie Card to remember the rule.**

Kimberly

Kimberly, an 11-year-old girl, hugs everyone she sees. As she is getting older, this behavior is appearing more and more inappropriate, and her parents are becoming increasingly concerned about it. They have tried a variety of interventions, but Kimberly continues to insist that she hug each and every person she encounters.

Kimberly loves country music singers, particularly Shania Twain. Using the Power Card strategy, Kimberly's parents were able to teach their daughter a more appropriate greeting.

Shania Twain Greets Her Fans
by Kitty Flinn

Shania Twain meets hundreds of people each year. After her concerts, she spends time with her fans, greeting them and autographing pictures. She used to hug all the people she met but then realized that this is not the only way, or the best way, to greet somebody she is meeting for the first time. Some people do not like to be hugged, especially by someone they are meeting for the first time. Just like Shania, it is important for everybody to learn to greet appropriately.

Shania is anxious to share these three key points that she has learned about greeting people:

1. *Smile and put out your right hand and shake the other person's right hand.*

2. *Introduce yourself and ask the person how they are.*

3. *Practice greetings with your friends and teachers.*

Following these steps will help you greet people just like Shania!!

1. **Smile and put out your right hand and shake the other person's right hand.**

2. **Introduce yourself and ask the person how they are.**

3. **Practice greetings with your friends and teachers.**

• • •

Regulation

Justin

The power of *Star Wars* was used to help 9-year-old Justin remember to use his self-calming strategy. Justin and his teacher created this scenario and Power Card together.

Yoda and Self-Calming

Yoda is the most powerful of all of the Jedi Masters. Sometimes Yoda gets frustrated when things are hard. When Yoda is frustrated, he takes a deep breath and he takes a break. I will try to be like Jedi Mater Yoda when I am frustrated!

When I am frustrated, I will:

- *Stay calm.*
- *Take two deep breaths.*
- *Ask to take a break.*

When I am frustrated I will stay calm just like Master Yoda!!

- **Stay calm.**
- **Take two deep breaths.**
- **Ask to take a break.**

Mark

Mark enjoyed reading children's storybooks and adamantly told his high school peers that his special interest was analyzing children's literature because he wanted to be a children's literature professor. Mark's school team had been working with him on projecting a positive attitude toward others and used this as one of the strategies to help him reach this goal.

The Little Engine That Could

In the children's classic book The Little Engine That Could *by Watty Piper, a small engine finds the strength to pull a long train. Despite his small size, the engine's positive attitude and perseverance allow him to complete a task that other engines were not able to accomplish.*

Like many other children's books, this book has a lesson for people of all ages. The lesson is that when people have a positive attitude and don't complain, they are able to accomplish anything. Even though The Little Engine had doubts, he did not express those doubts but forged ahead with the task at hand.

Research has shown that what we say has a direct result on how we feel. People who complain a lot are less likely to accomplish what they need to do. People who use positive body language and words are more successful.

The Little Engine has this advice:

1. *Greet people with a smile even when you don't feel like it. This will make them feel good and make you feel better as well.*

2. *If you think you can, you usually can.*

3. *If you think you can't, you won't try as hard, and this will usually lead to a negative outcome.*

Be like The Little Engine and say to yourself, "I think I can!"

1. **Greet people with a smile even when you don't feel like it. This will make them feel good and make you feel better as well.**

2. **If you think you can, you usually can.**

3. **If you think you can't, you won't try as hard and this will usually lead to a negative outcome.**

Tommy

Tommy sometimes becomes frustrated when he has difficulty completing his work. At times, he falls to the ground kicking and screaming and has difficulty regaining his composure. These meltdowns can last up to 45 minutes. Tommy loves baseball, particularly his hero, Cal Ripken Jr.

The following scenario and Power Card were introduced to Tommy to help him control his meltdowns.

How Cal Ripken Handles Frustration
by Kitty Flinn

Cal Ripken is one of the best baseball players of all times. He enjoyed playing for the Baltimore Orioles for 21 years. Cal understands that it is very important to work hard and stay focused on and off the field. However, there are times when Cal gets frustrated and feels like falling to the ground screaming. He realizes that this would be inappropriate. He knows that if he behaved this way, the umpire would throw him out of the game.

Cal wants everyone to know how important it is to handle frustrations appropriately. He began working on controlling his temper when he was in elementary school and has advice for all boys who feel frustrated.

The next time you begin to feel a little frustrated, try doing the following three things that helped Cal:

1. *Stop and take a deep breath.*

2. *Ask an adult if you can go to a quiet area to have a few minutes to calm down.*

3. *Talk to an adult, like a teacher, and work on a solution.*

Work on these rules and you will score a homerun in the classroom!

1. **Stop and take a deep breath.**

2. **Ask an adult if you can go to a quiet area to have a few minutes to calm down.**

3. **Talk to an adult, like a teacher, and work on a solution.**

• • •

School-Based Skills

Kito

To avoid completing assignments, Kito, a 10-year-old boy with ASD, repeatedly breaks his pencils and destroys erasers. Kito has a special interest in the television game show *Family Feud*, hosted by Steve Harvey. Kito enjoys playing the role of Steve Harvey and frequently plays the game with his younger brother and sister. This scenario and Power Card resulted in a decrease in the target behavior.

Steve Harvey and His Pencil
by Rachele M. Hill

When getting ready to host Family Feud, *Steve Harvey uses a pencil to prepare cards with information about each of his contestants. He has a limited amount of time to do this and knows that it is important to use his pencil wisely. He likes to keep his pencil all in one piece with a sharp point and a good eraser. He also keeps track of his pencil so it doesn't get lost.*

Mr. Harvey wants everyone to know how important it is to have a pencil that is long, sharp, and neat. He knows students in school need to have a good pencil every day. Mr. Harvey is always proud of students who are responsible for their long, sharp, and neat pencils.

Steve Harvey wants you to remember these three things:

1. *Keep your pencil in one piece.*

2. *Make sure your pencil always has a sharp point and a good eraser.*

3. Be responsible for keeping track of your pencil.

Try your best to remember these things and you will always be a winner in the classroom.

1. **Keep your pencil in one piece.**
2. **Make sure your pencil always has a sharp point and a good eraser.**
3. **Be responsible for keeping track of your pencil.**

Meghan

After 8-year-old Meghan completes her assignments, she loves drawing with markers on a piece of butcher paper. Unfortunately, she sometimes draws on the table as well as on her body. Besides, she is constantly losing the caps of her markers.

Meghan has a special interest in Barbie, often carrying her doll with her. She also enjoys discussing Barbie merchandise and looking at picture books with Barbie themes. The following scenario and Power Card were written to encourage Meghan to use markers appropriately.

Barbie and Her Markers
by Lisa Burch

When Barbie finishes her school assignments, she loves to draw with her many colorful markers. She has learned that it is important to take care of her markers so they last a long time. When she is getting ready to draw, she puts the marker cap on the opposite end of the marker so she won't lose it. She is always careful to draw only on the paper so her desk and body stay clean. When she is finished with a marker, she puts the cap back on right away. Barbie wants every girl and boy to take good care of their markers. She has learned that it is important to have markers with caps so her favorite colors don't dry up.

Barbie wants you to remember these three things:

1. Put the cap on the end of your marker before you draw.

2. Be careful to only draw on the paper.

3. Put the cap back on the marker when you are finished.

Try your best to remember these three things so you can draw just like Barbie!!

1. **Put the cap on the end of your marker before you draw.**

2. **Be careful to only draw on the paper.**

3. **Put the cap back on the marker when you are finished.**

Charlie

Charlie is a seventh grader who has a great deal of trouble with handwriting. Not only is his handwriting difficult to read, but Charlie becomes extremely agitated when he has to take notes in his classes. As a result, he often interrupts the teacher by blurting out statements such as, "Slow down!" or "You're talking so fast I can't keep up!"

Charlie is interested in Pokémon™ trading cards and enjoys discussing the Pokémon characters with his classmates. The following scenario and Power Card were created to help Charlie accept alternatives to taking handwritten notes in class.

Brock's Handwriting
by Carla Huhtanen

Writing is not an easy skill for many people. Many of our most admired professionals, such as doctors, lawyers, and even teachers, have problems with handwriting. Even Brock has difficulty putting legible letters on paper. Every week when he is away from home finding new Pokémon, he writes to his brothers and sisters. He is concerned that because of his handwriting, his family will not be able to enjoy reading about the many exciting adventures he is experiencing around the world.

Because of his concerns, Brock came up with three terrific solutions.

1. *Sometimes Brock uses his iPad to record his assignments.*

2. *Brock also uses an iPad to type his stories. He isn't very fast yet but that doesn't matter. Brock knows that the more he types, the faster he gets.*

3. *When his friend Ash is around, Brock dictates his words and Ash writes down every exciting detail.*

Just like Brock, other kids who have problems with handwriting can learn strategies to keep in touch with family and friends. Follow Brock's suggestions and you too can say what you want to say in writing!

1. **Sometimes Brock uses his iPad to record his assignments.**

2. **Brock also uses an iPad to type his stories. He isn't very fast yet but that doesn't matter. Brock knows that the more he types, the faster he gets.**

3. **When his friend Ash is around, Brock dictates his words and Ash writes down every exciting detail.**

Kelly

Kelly is a 15-year-old who does not enjoy riding the school bus. She often complains about the noisy brakes and becomes distressed when getting on and off the bus.

Kelly enjoys watching *The Rugrats* on television after school. After she was introduced to the Power Card strategy using one of the Rugrats, Kelly's teachers and parents saw an improvement in Kelly's behavior on the bus and less apprehension about the bus rides to and from school.

Angelica and the School Bus
by Kitty Flinn

Angelica can often be seen riding the school bus. She enjoys going to school and knows that riding the bus means getting a break from "those babies." What Angelica doesn't like about the bus are the noisy brakes, but she found a solution to the problem. Angelica now wears head-phones on the bus and listens to her favorite music all the way to school and back home again.

Just like Angelica, students everywhere can wear head-phones on the bus. It is lots of fun to listen to your favorite music or stories on the bus. Many children have found that when they enjoy the bus ride, it makes it easier to get on and off the bus.

Angelica would like for you to remember these three things:

1. When waiting for the bus, put on your earbuds and select a playlist.

2. Begin playing the music when you sit down on the bus.

3. Keep the earbuds in and the music going until you are off the bus.

Angelica is thrilled when students take her advice and wear earbuds on the bus!

1. **When waiting for the bus, put on your earbuds and select a playlist.**

2. **Begin playing the music when you sit down on the bus.**

3. **Keep the earbuds in and the music going until you are off the bus.**

SCHOOL BUS

STOP

Leslie

Thirteen-year-old Leslie loves classical music, and her goal is to be a part of a symphony orchestra when she is an adult. Leslie's difficulty in following directions prompted her paraprofessional to create a scenario and Power Card entitled "The Class Is Like a Symphony."

How a Classroom Is Like a Symphony
by Kathy Wadman and Lisa Farnsworth

The teacher in the classroom is like the conductor in the symphony. A conductor makes sure that all musicians are on the same page. It would be musical chaos if the violinists decided to play jazz when everyone else was playing Mozart!

In the classroom, students need to be on the same page. If the teacher tells the class to get math books out, then everyone (that means me too!) gets the math book out. The teacher will let us know what page we should be on. All students, just like musicians, have to be on the same page!

The teacher will give the directions. I must listen carefully! After the teacher has given directions, I will be given JUST ONE warning to follow directions.

When the musicians in a symphony follow the conductor and have a great performance, the audience claps and often yells, "Bravo!" If I do a good job of following directions, I'll get my work done easier and sooner, and I'll earn electronic time at home – maybe even at school – if I do a REALLY good job!

*However, if I ignore or choose not to follow the directions, I will not be able to stay with the symphony (the class). Instead, I will have a **"solo performance"** in the Navigator Room! The teacher or para will place the "Solo" card on my desk, which means that I must leave the classroom quietly and go to the Navigator Room with my work. Unfortunately, when that happens, I miss out on what's going on in class and also lose electronic time!*

This is a plan to help me become the best student I can be. It will take effect January 15. My mom and dad know about the plan and are in agreement with how it works.

I really enjoy music. I want to be part of the symphony (the class), so I will try extra hard to follow directions!

1. The teacher will give directions.

2. I must listen carefully.

3. If I follow the directions with 0 or 1 warning, I will get a symphony "bravo" and earn electronic time.

4. If I do not follow directions, I will earn a "solo performance" and no electronic time.

SOLO Performance Card.

Go quietly and directly to Navigator Room.

BRAVO!!! Performance Card.

Great job following directions!

You earned some extra technology time!

Sam

Sam is a highly intelligent sixth-grade student who hopes one day to attend Harvard and often speaks of this plan to anyone who is willing to listen. But even though Sam is intelligent, he has developed few organizational strategies. Specifically, he doesn't ask questions about course requirements and, therefore, often fails to turn in assignments on time.

The following scenario and Power Card were introduced to Sam by his mother to provide him with organizational strategies.

A Harvard Student
by Becky Heinrichs

Dave is proud to be a student at Harvard. He spent many hours studying throughout middle school and high school so he could achieve his dream. He always had difficulty with organization and relied on his mother to keep track of course requirements, paperwork, and due dates.

When Dave got to Harvard, he realized that he was having difficulty with organization. He scheduled a meeting with his English professor and explained his problems to him and received the following advice:

1. Take class notes and write all assignments in a calendar.

2. Ask questions when you don't understand.

3. Break down assignments into small steps, assign deadlines for each step, and write all deadlines and assignment due dates in a calendar.

You don't have to wait to get to Harvard to practice these three steps. Dave now knows that he would have enjoyed middle school and high school much more if he would have tried these things earlier.

1. **Take class notes and write all assignments in a calendar.**

2. **Ask questions when you don't understand.**

3. **Break down assignments into small steps, assign deadlines for each step, and write all deadlines and assignment due dates in a calendar.**

• • •

Home-Based Skills

Melody

Eight-year-old Melody has always slept with her parents, sister, or brother despite lots of efforts by her parents to change this behavior over the years. After attending a workshop on the Power Card strategy, Melody's mother, hoping that this might be a helpful strategy for their family, approached Melody's teacher about helping her write a scenario and a Power Card. They decided to feature Melody's special interest, Katy Perry.

Katy Perry Sleeps by Herself
by Kathy Wadman

When Katy Perry was 8 years old, she was afraid to sleep by herself. She heard noises that scared her. Sometimes she slept with her sister or her brother.

Katy's brother and sister did not sleep well when Katy slept with them. They would be tired and cranky the next day. Katy would be tired, too!

One day, Katy did some thinking. She thought about these things:

- *I am 8 years old, and, I am a big girl.*

- *All my friends sleep in their own beds.*

- *I am tired of being tired all the time.*

So Katy decided she would sleep in her own bed. She was afraid at first. Katy kept telling herself, "I can do it. I can do it!"

When Katy went to bed, she plumped up her pillow and fixed her sheets and blankets just right, and she got her favorite stuffed animals in bed with her. She got into her comfy bed and said, "I am tired."

She turned on her iPod to listen to some of her favorite music. She loves to listen to Beyoncé and Adele! She also likes to listen to her own songs. Her favorite is "Fireworks" because she used to be afraid of fireworks noises. But one day she decided not to be afraid any more and she said, "I'm going to write a song about fireworks because I am not afraid of those noises any more. They are just loud noises."

Katy went to bed and closed her eyes and listened to her music. She thought about candy, swimming, and her stuffed animals. She remembered that she was going to be brave.

The next morning, Katy woke up in her own bed! She felt so proud of herself. She did it! She was so happy that she started to sing. And she noticed that her singing was better! She did not feel tired! Her brother and sister were not tired either. Her mom and dad were very proud of her being so brave!

Katy Perry loves to sleep in her own bed. She likes that it is cozy and she has her stuffed animals and her iPod. I can sleep in my own bed like Katy Perry. I can be brave just like Katy Perry. My mom and dad, and Ms. Wadman, will be proud of me! I can do it – just like Katy Perry!

1. **Fix your bed just right.**
2. **Get your stuffed animals.**
3. **Turn on your music.**
4. **Get in bed.**
5. **Close your eyes and say, "I'm tired."**

Jennifer

Jennifer is a second-grade student who has acquired many social skills, such as initiating a conversation and introducing visitors to the class. In addition, she independently uses the school restroom. However, Jennifer consistently forgets to wash her hands after using the toilet.

Jennifer's teacher wrote the following scenario and Power Card featuring Angelica from Jennifer's favorite cartoon, *The Rugrats*, to remind her to wash her hands. An enlarged copy of Jennifer's Power Card was placed in the bathroom to remind her of the proper steps to hand washing.

Angelica Says, "Wash Those Hands"
by Rachele M. Hill

Angelica knows how important it is to keep her hands clean. She does not want to catch any yucky germs from "those babies!" Germs can cause coughing, sneezing, and runny noses. Angelica definitely does not want to catch a cold! She washes her hands often and always after using the bathroom. She knows that washing her hands helps avoid catching a cold.

Angelica wants you to have clean hands, too. She wants you to remember to wash your hands often, and every time after you go to the bathroom. Angelica wants you to remember these three things:

1. *Wash your hands after you go to the bathroom.*
2. *Always use soap.*
3. *Dry your hands completely.*

Angelica can be very bossy, but she does have manners when it comes to having clean hands. Angelica says, "Please wash your hands!"

1. **Wash your hands after you go to the bathroom.**
2. **Always use soap.**
3. **Dry your hands completely.**

John

John, an 8-year-old boy, does not go to the bathroom unless someone reminds him. As a result, he sometimes wets his pants and then becomes angry with his mother or teacher because they did not remind him to go to the bathroom.

John's favorite cartoon character is Superman, and he enjoys pretending that he is Superman or Clark Kent. The following scenario and Power Card were introduced to John to encourage him to use the bathroom independently.

Superman and the Bathroom
by Kitty Flinn

During his many flights to help people in need, Superman has found it necessary to stop and use the bathroom once in a while. He knows it is important to go when he needs to, and he doesn't wait for someone to ask him if he has to go. He knows that it is important for superheroes to take care of their bathroom needs on their own.

Superman would like for you to consider these three facts:

1. *When you are at home, don't wait for someone to ask if you need to go to the bathroom. Just go when you need to go.*

2. *When you are at school, tell your teacher that you need to go to the bathroom. Try and go every time there is a scheduled break, even if you don't feel you need to.*

3. *If you are away from home, tell an adult you are with that you need to use the bathroom and have them show you where it is located.*

Superman is proud of young men who can take care of their bathroom needs on their own.

1. When you are at home, don't wait for someone to ask if you need to go to the bathroom. Just go when you need to go.

2. When you are at school, tell your teacher that you need to go to the bathroom. Try and go every time there is a scheduled break, even if you don't feel you need to.

3. If you are away from home, tell an adult you are with that you need to use the bathroom and have them show you where it is located.

Jeremy

Jeremy, a 9-year-old with high-functioning autism, often refuses to go to bed at night, leaving him exhausted at school the next day. His parents feel they have tried everything. Jeremy's classroom teacher has arranged for Jeremy to e-mail a local firefighter on a regular basis after he has completed academic tasks at school. This has proven to be a powerful reinforcer for Jeremy, who has a huge interest in firefighting and often talks about becoming a firefighter when he grows up.

Using the following scenario and Power Card helped Jeremy understand the importance of a full night's sleep and consequently helped him go to bed without a struggle. He even took his Power Card to bed with him at night.

Firefighter Steve Goes to Bed
by Nicole Rahaim

Firefighter Steve really enjoys being a firefighter. Sometimes he gets back to the firehouse after a fire and has trouble going to sleep. He thinks that it might be more fun to stay up and watch television or talk with the other firefighters, but he knows he needs his sleep. He knows that it is important to get a good night's sleep so he will be rested and do a good job when there is another fire.

It is important for all future firefighters to learn to get a good night's sleep when they are young. Firefighter Steve has learned to do these three things when he has trouble going to bed:

1. *Follow a bedtime routine. Firefighter Steve takes a bath, brushes his teeth, and reads for 15 minutes before turning off the light.*
2. *Close your eyes and try to lie still.*
3. *Stay in bed after the lights are out.*

Firefighters Steve is proud of young men who get plenty of rest every night. He knows that they will make great firefighters some day!

1. **Follow a bedtime routine. Firefighter Steve takes a bath, brushes his teeth, and reads for 15 minutes before turning off the light.**

2. **Close your eyes and try to lie still.**

3. **Stay in bed after the lights are out.**

• • •

Summary

The examples in this chapter demonstrate how the Power Card strategy can address myriad skill areas for individuals with ASD who have a special interest. This evidence-based strategy is highly motivating and easily adaptable for school-age learners.

CHAPTER 4

Using the Power Card Strategy to Increase Academic Performance

With Kathy Wadman

Variations of the Power Card strategy can be used in multiple ways. For example, it can be used as a basis for a modified curriculum for students with ASD. In fact, because it is built around the student's special interest, the Power Card strategy may result in increased academic progress.

• • •

Andrew

Andrew, a 10-year-old with ASD, has a special interest in law enforcement but is discouraged from discussing this at school because his teacher and his parents fear that by being so focused on this one topic, he will not be able to complete his assignments. Andrew spends his days thinking about law enforcement, and although he is reprimanded each time he brings up the subject, he doesn't stop daydreaming about cops and robbers or replaying police movies in his mind. Andrew seldom completes assignments and has no friends. Despite an above-average IQ, his grades are well below average, and getting him to attend school is a daily struggle.

Andrew is also difficult to motivate. Typically, he does not respond to the kinds of reinforcement systems that are effective for other students in his class. For example, Miss Newman gives extra minutes of recess when students complete assignments in a timely fashion. The rest of the class loves this incentive, but Andrew hates recess and does everything he can think of to sabotage other students so they won't get extra time on the playground. Needless to say, such behavior further distances him from his peers.

Andrew is typical of many children with ASD in that his area of interest is obvious. However, this is not the case with everybody. In those instances where an area of interest is not easily identified, there are three primary ways to obtain this information:

- by observing the student during unstructured time (i.e., free-choice time, play time, recess, break time)

- through informal conversation with the student

- by completing an interest inventory or reinforcement survey. (You typically do not need to have the student complete an interest inventory or reinforcement preference survey to identify the special interest.)

Once the area of interest has been determined, it is beneficial for those who support the learner to brainstorm ways to incorporate the area of interest into the curriculum and all other aspects of the school day. Throughout this process, it is important for the team to consider the special interest as a strength that can be used to the learner's benefit rather than to view it as a liability that needs to be eliminated. This is not to say that the student should be allowed to spend all of his time obsessing about his interest. Rather, the special interest is used to spark an interest in curriculum, encourage task completion, and improve behavior. As with all interventions, it is important to collect data to determine the success of the intervention.

In the rest of this chapter we will look at three children with ASD and analyze how their special interests were turned into an asset to improve their academic performance.

• • •

Kanisha

Kanisha is a delightful 8-year-old with a diagnosis of ASD. She spends one period of her school day in a special education resource room and the remainder of the time in a second-grade general education classroom. Her services include the support of an instructional assistant for the general education classroom, as needed, and direct instruction in the resource room for written language arts.

Initially, developing a curriculum for Kanisha proved difficult. Her short attention span and limited verbal language made it almost impossible to measure her reading comprehension. In addition, her apparent lack of interest in anything academic compounded the situation. However, it was determined that Kanisha had a strong interest in dogs as she often mentioned her dog, Fly. As a result, she was encouraged to talk about her dog with those who worked with her during social skills training as well as during unstructured time. Gradually, it became clear that using this topic could be key to Kanisha's academic and social success. As a result, the following tasks were incorporated into Kanisha's day:

- **Encourage Kanisha to ask other people about their dogs.** This became Kanisha's way to initiate conversation with adults and peers. At first Kanisha would ask, "Do you have a dog?" Later this was expanded to asking specific questions about the dog such as, "What type of dog do you have?," "What color is your dog?," and so on. A Power Card provided visual support by reminding Kanisha of appropriate questions to ask.

- **Create a picture book of different kinds of dogs.** As a start, pictures of dogs were cut out of magazines or downloaded from the Internet. Soon, those who knew Kanisha brought photographs of their dogs to be included in the book. Kanisha also added written text to the book describing the dogs, thereby providing handwriting and keyboarding practice. Further, Kanisha looked at the picture book with adults and peers during free time and used the pictures to initiate conversation. Finally, the picture book was used as a reinforcer – Kanisha was motivated to complete assignments so she could look at the picture book.

- **Adapt Kanisha's curriculum to incorporate her interest in dogs.** Whenever possible, Kanisha 's curriculum was modified to include her area of interest. For example, math word problems included references to dogs, and reading included stories about dogs.

Encouraging Kanisha's interest in dogs allowed her the opportunity to make academic gains, increased her time on task, and improved her ability to communicate. It also improved her social status among her peers, as the other second graders regarded Kanisha as "the expert on dogs."

• • •

Jeffrey

Jeffrey, a third grader on the spectrum, spends the majority of his school day in the general education classroom. His learning opportunities are hindered by distractibility, lack of sustained attention, and disorganization. Difficulties with gross- and fine-motor tasks further complicate his school day, particularly when he is required to complete written assignments or expected to participate in organized large-group activities in physical education or at recess.

Math and language arts are especially challenging for Jeffrey. In math, he experiences difficulty with number recall and computation. In written language, he tends to stray off the topic or become lost in his thoughts and constant daydreaming.

Through observation, his resource room teacher determined that Jeffrey was very interested in the World Wrestling Federation and also in a variety of imaginary characters he created related to wrestling. However, Jeffrey had poor social skills and was unable to connect with his peers.

The following modifications were provided for Jeffrey:

- **Incorporate World Wrestling Entertainment (WWE) characters into Jeffrey's math lessons**. Jeffrey and his teacher assigned a wrestler to each numeral (for example, Kane was number 7, and The Rock was number 8), and Jeffrey created a story for each math fact. When recalling the sum of 7 x 8, Jeffrey would recall the story he had created as well as the math fact. Although this appeared complex to his teacher, it was an excellent memory aid for Jeffrey. His motivation increased, and he was eager to create new vignettes.

- **Incorporate WWE into the algorithm of double-digit multiplication**. Jeffrey experienced difficulty with recall until double-digit multiplication became a tag team wrestling bout. For example, the problem 55 x 32 became the "five" brothers against the team of "three and two."

- **Use the WWE characters to "breathe life" into story problems**. It was easy to change names in story problems to those of members of the WWE. This simple strategy made a remarkable difference in Jeffrey's motivation.

- **Allow Jeffrey to incorporate wrestling characters into creative writing and research projects.** For example, the make-believe wrestling character "Doink" became the epitome of the Florida tourist in his research paper on "The Animals of Florida."

- **Use the Power Card Strategy to address Jeffrey's social skill concerns.** The scenario and Power Card developed for Jeffrey used WWE characters and provided information related to initiating and sustaining a conversation.

Incorporating special interests into his school day decreased Jeffrey's stress level and enabled him to focus better on academic topics. In addition, other students began to view him as an intelligent and highly original thinker. As peers began to see him in a positive light, Jeffrey's self-esteem improved.

• • •

Matt

Matt, a first-grade student with ASD, has a near-obsessive interest in fairytales. He is making little academic progress. By January of his first-grade year, Matt is already behind his peers in reading, and his classroom teacher considers him a nonreader. Like many children with ASD, Matt does not have the emotional resources to cope with classroom demands, is easily stressed, and cannot tolerate making mistakes. Not surprisingly, his behavioral outbursts, off-task behavior, and difficulty following directions interfere with his ability to learn. His teachers can almost always predict when a meltdown is about to occur because Matt starts rubbing his hands on his jeans.

The following modifications were provided for Matt:

- **Use the Power Card Strategy to address Matt's stress and frustration**. Matt, whose interest in fairytales included *Jack and the Beanstalk*, became more focused in the classroom when presented with a Power Card featuring "Jack."

- **Provide Matt the opportunity to dictate fairytales.**
  A variation of a language-experience approach was
  used that provided Matt the opportunity to dictate
  stories to his teacher. Matt added illustrations and
  was anxious to "read" the completed story to his
  teacher. Once the topical interest was incorporated, he demonstrated a remarkable ability to recall
  words. Phonics instruction was added at a later
  date, and Matt currently reads above grade level.

- **Allow Matt to use reading as a free-time activity.**
  Since Matt often chose solitary activities and his
  peer interactions were limited, providing him with
  preferred reading material proved to be calming to
  him. On occasion, Matt would read fairytales with
  other children in the class.

- **Allow Matt to draw during instructional time**. At
  first glance, it appeared that Matt was not paying
  attention to what was going on around him while
  he was drawing, but in reality his comprehension
  improved when he was permitted to draw. Not surprisingly, his drawings always reflected his topic of
  interest.

- **Allow Matt to choose topics for written work.** Simply allowing Matt to choose his topic reduced frustration and refusals to work. This, in turn, reduced
  power struggles and confrontations, and the quality
  of his work improved.

• • •

Summary

Creative educators and parents know the value of tapping into the strengths of individuals with ASD. Many children and adolescents with ASD can be difficult to motivate, but using an area of interest is often the key to improved behavior and academic success. Whether using the Power Card strategy, adapting curriculum to reflect the student's interest, or a combination of both, using a special interest is a low-cost, effective and positive behavioral support.

References

American Psychiatric Association. (2013). *Diagnostic and statistical manual of mental disorders – 5th edition*. Washington, DC: Author

Angell, M. E., Nicholson, J. K., Watts, E. H., & Blum, C. T. (2011). Using a multicomponent adapted Power Card strategy to decrease latency during interactivity transitions for three children with developmental disabilities. *Focus on Autism and Other Developmental Disabilities, 26*(4), 206-217.

Asperger, H. (1991). Die "Autistischen Psychopathen" im Kindersalter. In U. Frith (Ed. & Trans.), *Autism and Asperger syndrome* (pp. 37-92). New York, NY: Cambridge University Press. (Original work published 1944).

Aspy, G. R., Grossman, B. G., Myles, B. S., & Henry, S. A. (2016). *FBA to Z: Functional behavior assessment and intervention plans for individuals with autism spectrum disorder.* Shawnee Mission, KS: AAPC Publishing.

Barber, A. B., Saffo, R. W., Gilpin, A. T., Craft, L. D., & Goldstein, H. (2016). Peers as clinicians: Examining the impact of Stay Play Talk on social communication in young preschoolers with autism. *Journal of Communication Disorders, 59*, 1-15.

Bashe, P. R., & Kirby, B. L. (2010). *The OASIS guide to Asperger syndrome: Completely revised and updated: Advice, support, insight, and inspiration.* New York, NY: Crown Publishers.

Bishop-Fitzpatrick, L., Minshew, N. J., & Eack, S. M. (2014). A systematic review of psychosocial interventions for adults with autism spectrum disorders. In F. R. Volkmar, B. Reichow, & J. McPhartland (Eds.), *Adolescents and adults with autism spectrum disorders* (pp. 315-327). New York, NY: Springer.

*Boyd, B. A., Conroy, M. A., Mancil, G. R., Nakao, T., & Alter, P. J. (2007). Effects of circumscribed interests on the social behaviors of children with autism spectrum disorders. *Journal of Autism and Developmental Disorders, 37*(8), 1550-1561.

*Campbell, A., & Tincani, M. (2011). The Power Card strategy: Strength-based intervention to increase direction following of children with autism spectrum disorder. *Journal of Positive Behavior Interventions, 13*, 240-249.

Cascio, C. J., Foss-Feig, J. H., Heavock, J., Schauder, K. B., Loring, W. A., Rogers, B. P., Pryweller, J. R., Newsom, C. R., Cockren, J., Cao, A., & Bolton, S. (2014). Affective neural response to restricted interests in autism spectrum disorders. *The Journal of Child Psychology and Psychiatry, 55*(2), 162-171.

Case-Smith, J., Weaver, L. L., & Fristad, M. A. (2014). A systematic review of sensory processing interventions for children with autism spectrum disorders. *Autism.* doi:10.1177/1362361313517762

Centers for Medicare and Medicaid Services. (2010). *Autism spectrum disorders: Final report on environmental scan.* Washington, DC: Author.

Daubert, A., Hornstein, S., & Tincani, M. (2015). Effects of a modified Power Card strategy on turn taking and social commenting of children with autism spectrum disorder playing board games. *Journal of Developmental and Physical Disabilities, 27*(1), 93-110.

*Davis, K., Boon, R., Cihak, D., & Fore, C. (2010). Power Cards to improve conversational skills in adolescents with Asperger syndrome. *Focus on Autism and Other Developmental Disabilities, 25,* 12-22.

DeLoache, J. S., Simcock, G., & Macari, S. (2007). Planes, trains, automobiles – and tea sets: Extremely intense interests in very young children. *Developmental Psychology, 43,* 1579-1586.

Dichter, G.S., Felder, J.N., Green, S.R., Rittenberg, A.M., Sasson, N.J., & Bodfish, J.W. (2012). Reward circuitry function in autism spectrum disorders. *Social Cognitive and Affective Neuroscience, 7,* 160–172.

*Dunst, C. J., Trivette, C. M., & Masiello, T. (2011). Exploratory investigation of the effects of interest-based learning on the development of young children with autism. *Autism, 15*(3), 295-305.

Durand, V. M., & Crimmins, D. (1992). *Motivation assessment scale.* Topeka, KS: Monaco & Associates.

*El Zein, F., Solis, M., Lang, R., & Kim, M. K. (2014). Embedding perseverative interest of a child with autism in text may result in improved reading comprehension: A pilot study. *Developmental Neurorehabilitation,* 1-5.

Fecteau, S., Mottron, L., Berthiaume, C., & Burack, J. A. (2003). Developmental changes of autistic symptoms. *Autism, 7*(3), 255-268.

*Gunn, K. C., & Delafield-Butt, J. T. (2015). Teaching children with autism spectrum disorder with restricted interests: A review of evidence for best practice. *Review of Educational Research*, 1-23. doi:0034654315604027

Hampshire, P. K., Butera, G. D., & Bellini, S. (2016) Self-management and parents as interventionists to improve homework independence in students with autism spectrum disorders. *Preventing School Failure: Alternative Education for Children and Youth, 60*(1), 22-34.

Jordan, C. J., & Caldwell-Harris, C. L. (2012). Understanding differences in neurotypical and autism spectrum special interests through Internet forums. *Intellectual and Developmental Disabilities, 50*(5), 391-402.

*Jung, S., & Sainato, D. M. (2015). Teaching games to young children with autism spectrum disorder using special interests and video modelling. *Journal of Intellectual and Developmental Disability, 40*(2), 198-212.

Kasari, C., Dean, M., Kretzmann, M., Shih, W., Orlich, F., Whitney, R., ... & King, B. (2016). Children with autism spectrum disorder and social skills groups at school: A randomized trial comparing intervention approach and peer composition. *Journal of Child Psychology and Psychiatry, 57*(2), 171-179.

*Keeling, K., Myles, B., Gagnon, E., & Simpson, R. (2003). Using the Power Card strategy to teach sportsmanship skills to a child with autism. *Focus on Autism and Other Developmental Disabilities, 18*, 105-111.

Kern, L., Dunlap, G., Clarke, S., & Childs, K. (1994). Student-assisted functional assessment interview. *Diagnostique, 19*(2-3), 29-39.

Kirchner, J. C. & Dziobek, I. (2014). Toward the successful employment of adults with autism: A first analysis of special interests and factors deemed important for vocational performance. *Scandinavian Journal of Child and Adolescent Psychiatry and Psychology, 2*(2) 77-85.

Klin, A., Danovitch, J. H., Merz, A. B., & Volkmar, F. R. (2007). Circumscribed interests in higher functioning individuals with autism spectrum disorders: An exploratory study. *Research & Practice for Persons with Severe Disabilities, 32*(2), 89-100.

Knight, V., Sartini, E., & Spriggs, A. D. (2015). Evaluating visual activity schedules as evidence-based practice for individuals with autism spectrum disorders. *Journal of Autism and Developmental Disorders, 45*(1), 157-178.

*Koegel, R., Kim, S., Koegel, L., & Schwartzman, B. (2013). Improving socialization for high school students with ASD by using their preferred interests. *Journal of Autism and Developmental Disorders, 43*, 2121-2134.

*Koegel, K. K., Singh, A. K., & Koegel, R. L. (2010). Improving motivation for academics in children with autism. *Journal of Autism and Developmental Disorders, 40*, 1057-1066.

*Kryzak, L. A., Bauer, S., Jones, E. A., & Sturmey, P. (2013). Increasing responding to others' joint attention directives using circumscribed interests. *Journal of Applied Behavior Analysis, 46*, 674-679.

*Lanou, A., Hough, L., & Powell, E. (2012). Case studies on using special interests to address the needs of students with autism spectrum disorders. *Intervention in School and Clinic, 47*(3), 175-182.

*Mancil, G., & Pearl, C. (2008). Restricted interests as motivators: Improving academic engagement and outcomes of children on the autism spectrum. *TEACHING Exceptional Children Plus, 4*(6), 2-15.

Matson, J. L., & Nebel-Schwalm, M. (2007). Assessing challenging behaviors in children with autism spectrum disorders: A review. *Research in Developmental Disabilities, 28*(6), 567-579.

Mercier, C., Mottron, L., & Belleville, S. (2000). A psychosocial study on restricted interests in high-functioning persons with pervasive developmental disorders. *Autism, 4*(4), 406-425.

Mesibov, G. B., & Shea, V. (2010). The TEACCH program in the era of evidence-based practice. *Journal of Autism and Developmental Disorders, 40*(5), 570-579.

Myles, B. S., & Aspy, R. (2016). *High-functioning autism and difficult moments: Practical solutions for meltdowns.* Shawnee Missions, KS: AAPC Publishing.

Myles, B. S., & Simpson, R. L. (2003). *Asperger Syndrome: A guide for educators and parents* (2nd ed.). Austin, TX: Pro-Ed.

Myles, B. S., Endow, J., & Mayfield, M. (2013). *The hidden curriculum of getting and keeping a job: Navigating the social landscape of employment. A guide for individuals with autism spectrum disorders and other social-cognitive challenges.* Shawnee Mission, KS: AAPC Publishing.

Myles, B. S., Trautman, M. L., & Schelvan, R. L. (2013). *The hidden curriculum: Practical solutions for understanding unstated rules in social situations* (2nd ed.). Shawnee Mission, KS: AAPC Publishing.

Myles, H. M., & Kolar, A. (2013). *The hidden curriculum and other practical solutions to everyday challenges for elementary-age children with high-functioning autism spectrum disorders* (2nd ed.). Shawnee Mission, KS: AAPC Publishing.

National Autism Center. (2015). *National standards project: Phase 2.* Retrieved from http://www.nationalautismcenter.org/national-standards-project/phase-2/

National Professional Development Center on Autism Spectrum Disorders. (n.d.). *Evidence-based practice briefs.* Retrieved from http://autismpdc.fpg.unc.edu/evidence-based-practices

Porter, N. (2012). Promotion of pretend play for children with high-functioning autism through the use of circumscribed interests. *Early Childhood Education Journal, 40,* 161-167.

Reese, R. M., Richman, D. M., Belmont, J. M., & Morse, P. (2005). Functional characteristics of disruptive behavior in developmentally disabled children with and without autism. *Journal of Autism and Developmental Disorders, 35*(4), 419-428.

*Sasson, N. J., Elison, J. T., Turner-Brown, L. M., Dichter, G. S., & Bodfish, J. W. (2011). Brief report: Circumscribed attention in young children with autism. *Journal of Autism and Developmental Disorders, 41*(2), 242-247.

*Spencer, V., Simpson, C., Day, M., & Buster, E. (2008). Using the Power Card strategy to teach social skills to a child with autism. *TEACHING Exceptional Children Plus, 5*(1), 1-10.

Turner-Brown, L. M., Lam, K. S., Holtzclaw, T. N., Dichter, G. S., & Bodfish, J. W. (2011). Phenomenology and measurement of circumscribed interests in autism spectrum disorders. *Autism, 15,* 437-456.

Virués-Ortega, J. (2010). Applied behavior analytic intervention for autism in early childhood: Meta-analysis, meta-regression and dose-response meta-analysis of multiple outcomes. *Clinical Psychology Review, 30*(4), 387-399.

*Vismara, L. A., & Lyons, G. L. (2007). Using perseverative interests to elicit joint attention behaviors in young children with autism. *Journal of Positive Behavior Interventions, 9,* 214-228.

Watkins, L., Kuhn, M., Ledbetter-Cho, K., Gevarter, C., & O'Reilly, M. (2015). Evidence-based social communication interventions for children with autism spectrum disorder. *The Indian Journal of Pediatrics*, 1-8.

White, P. J., O'Reilly, M., Streusand, W., Levine, A., Sigafoos, J., Lancioni, G., ... & Aguilar, J. (2011). Best practices for teaching joint attention: A systematic review of the intervention literature. *Research in Autism Spectrum Disorders, 5*(4), 1283-1295.

*Winter-Messiers, M. (2007). From tarantulas to toilet brushes: Understanding the special interest areas of children and youth with Asperger's syndrome. *Remedial and Special Education, 28*, 140-152.

Winter-Messiers, M. A., Herr, C. M., Wood, C. E., Brooks, A. P., Gates, M. A. M., Houston, T. L., & Tingstad, K. I. (2007). How far can Brian ride the Daylight 4449 Express: A strength-based model of Asperger syndrome based on special interest areas. *Focus on Autism and Other Developmental Disabilities, 22*(2), 67-79.

*Wood, J. J., Drahota, A., Sze, K., Har, K., Chiu, A., & Langer, D. A. (2009). Cognitive behavioral therapy for anxiety in children with autism spectrum disorders: A randomized, controlled trial. *Journal of Child Psychology and Psychiatry, 50*(3), 224-234.

Wright, B., Marshall, D., Adamson, J., Ainsworth, H., Ali, S., Allgar, V., ... & McMillan, D. (2016). Social Stories™ to alleviate challenging behaviour and social difficulties exhibited by children with autism spectrum disorder in mainstream schools: Design of a manualised training toolkit and feasibility study for a cluster randomised controlled trial with nested qualitative and cost-effectiveness components. *Health Technology Assessment (Winchester, England), 20*(6), 1-258.

Related books from AAPC

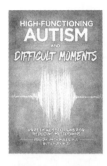

High-Functioning Autism and Difficult Moments: Practical Solutions for Reducing Meltdowns

Brenda Smith Myles, Ph.D., and Ruth Aspy, Ph.D.

**FBA to Z
Functional Behavior and Intervention Plans for Individuals With ASD**

Not just another book on traditional FBA approaches!

Ruth Aspy, Ph.D., Barry G. Grossman, Ph.D., Brenda Smith Myles, Ph.D., and Shawn A. Henry, M.S.

The Hidden Curriculum and Other Everyday Challenges for Elementary-Age Children With High-Functioning Autism

Haley Morgan Myles and Annellise Kolar

The Hidden Curriculum for Understanding Unstated rules in Social Situations for Adolescents and Young Adults

Brenda Smith Myles, Ph.D., Melissa L. Trautman, Ms.Ed., and Ronda L. Schelvan, Ms.Ed.

To order, visit AAPC at
www.aapcpublishing.net

11209 Strang Line Rd.
Lenexa, Kansas 66215
www.aapcpublishing.net

CPSIA information can be obtained
at www.ICGtesting.com
Printed in the USA
LVOW07s0803231017
553427LV00013B/689/P